THOMASTON, CT:

A Small Town Adventure in One Day

Bristol Street Press

Bristol Street Press

Thomaston, CT

Bristolstreetpress.com

ISBN: 978-1-7373769-2-7

DEDICATION

Dedicated to the wonderful citizens and business owners of Thomaston, Connecticut

CONTENTS

"Here in New England, the character is strong and unshakable."

— Norman Rockwell

Welcome to

Thomaston, CT.

SETH THOMAS FACTORY

Thomaston, Connecticut is located in the Northwest portion of the state, and while Thomaston is one of the smallest towns in Connecticut, it offers a lot to residents and day-trippers alike. Home to the famous Seth Thomas clock manufacturer, Thomaston has roots in nineteenth-century clockmaking. In fact, the main Seth Thomas factory is still standing and can be seen in the center of the town.

Originally named "Plymouth Hollow," Thomaston separated from the town Plymouth when Seth Thomas began labeling his clocks "Thomas Town." As of 1875, Thomas Town became Thomaston, and the Seth Thomas clock factory remained open for business until the late 1970s. The main factory is now home to smaller modern businesses and is an everyday reminder of the wonderful and unique history of the town.

In a modern era, Thomaston still retains a small-town industrial feeling. Because of its small size, visitors are often surprised to learn that there is much to do here. And the best part about visiting? The parks, businesses, and sites are all family-friendly with an emphasis on nature, activity, and fun. From the historical Thomaston Opera House to the Railroad Museum of New England, you can easily spend a day in the town and leave feeling as though you've traveled back in time.

This guidebook will lead you through some of the wonderful sites, parks, events, and historical locations in Thomaston. At the end of the guidebook, you will also find a list of surrounding area activities. These include the beautiful Plymouth Reservoir (right on the line between Plymouth and Thomaston), and the stores of Litchfield Center, only a ten-minute drive from Thomaston into Litchfield, CT.

The Thomaston Opera House

Built in 1884, The Thomaston Opera House is a gorgeous Victorian building located on Main Street in the heart of Thomaston. It hosts many live shows, including Elf, The Sound of Music, and Rudolph the Red-Nosed Reindeer, a musical. Even if you are not coming to watch a show, just touring the inside of the historical building is worth the trip. During the town's Light up Thomaston event in November, The Thomaston Opera House sparkles with many white Christmas lights, adding to its charm and beauty.

THE THOMASTON OPERA HOUSE ~ LIGHT UP THOMASTON

Website: landmarkcommunitytheatre.org

Directions: Route 8 South, Exit 40, right off exit, Main Street

Route 8 North, Exit 39, left at stop sign, Main Street

The Thomaston Dam

Driving over the Thomaston Dam feels like being on an amusement park ride. As you travel the short distance to the entrance, enjoy the scenic views, including trees, hills, water, and railroad tracks (from the many train voyages out of The Railroad Museum of New England). Pictures do not do the Thomaston Dam justice. It is a marvel that you must experience for yourself, in real life. On an autumn day, it is easily one of the most beautiful and picturesque locations in New England.

THE THOMASTON DAM

One of Connecticut's hidden gems, the Thomaston Dam was built in 1960 and remains a popular area for walking, sightseeing, photography, and biking. There is also a picnic area near the main entrance, so bring along your picnic baskets and hot dogs (grills and tables are provided at the site).

Hours of operation are subject to water levels, although the dam is usually open for walking along the main area May-September.

Website: nae.usace.army.mil/Missions/Recreation/Thomaston-Dam/

Directions: Route 8 North, Exit 39, left onto East Main Street, turn right at light onto North Main Street, turn right on Route 222, **331 Hill Rd. Thomaston, CT**

Black Rock Park

As soon as you drive into Black Rock Park (right over the line Thomaston/Watertown) you are presented with quite a few options. You can head to the beach area for water views, swimming, and picnicking, you can park beside the field and enjoy a game of frisbee, or you can drive straight through and opt for hiking the scenic trails. One particular area of interest is the bridge, which is a wonderful spot for taking autumn pictures of the family.

BLACK ROCK PARK

Camping is also available at Black Rock State Park May-September

Website: https://portal.ct.gov/DEEP/State-Parks/Parks/Black-Rock-State-Park

Directions:Route 8 North, Exit 38, left off exit, left at traffic light onto US ROUTE 6 west

Route 8 South, Exit 38, straight onto US ROUTE 6 west

Railroad Museum of New England

Because Thomaston is a small town, many residents can hear the train's whistle from inside their homes when the train journeys out. The historical train station, in Thomaston since 1881, offers rides in vintage passenger coaches! There are quite a few different and exciting types of journeys to choose from, including fall foliage, the Chocolate Decadence Tour, Easter Bunny ride, and the Santa Express. Please see the website for a full schedule and ticket purchasing options.

TRAIN VISITING THE THOMASTON DAM

Website: rmne.org

Directions:

Route 8 North, Exit 38, left off ramp, continue through center of town, bearing right, use ramp down to train station.

Route 8 South, Exit 40, right off exit, continue through center of town, turn left at light, use ramp down to train station

The Railroad Museum of New England is located at 242 E Main St. Thomaston, CT.

The Seth Thomas Factory and Seth Thomas House

The Seth Thomas Factory is still standing in Thomaston and is located right on Main Street in the center of town. You will notice it right away with its factory appearance and towering clock. The factory is now home to modern businesses, so be sure to check out their offerings!

SETH THOMAS FACTORY

Nearby is the Seth Thomas House, which is open for self-led tours during the town's Light up Thomaston event in November, and also available for full tours on Saturdays May, June, September, and October.

SETH THOMAS HOUSE

Please make plans in advance to view the house/museum. The factory is open business hours.

SETH THOMAS HOUSE INTERIOR

Factory Website: historicbuildingsct.com/seth-thomas-clock-factory-1915/

Seth Thomas House Website: thomastonct.org/content/165/272/default.aspx

Directions: Route 8 South, Exit 40, right off exit, Main Street

Route 8 North, Exit 39, left at stop sign, Main Street

Seth Thomas/Bradstreet House: 237 Main Street Thomaston, CT.

Seth Thomas Factory Building: 135 South Main Street Thomaston, CT.

Northfield Brook Lake

(Northfield Dam)

Gather up your picnic baskets for a trip to Northfield Brook Lake. With scenic views, picnic tables, lakes and streams, and even a wishing well for family photos, the Northfield Brook Lake and dam area is not to be missed. There are even horseshoe pits, grills, and hiking trails! You can easily spend your whole day or just your day-trip lunch hour here at the lake. Come spend some time with wildlife and relax in nature.

NORTHFIELD BROOK LAKE

Website: nae.usace.army.mil/Missions/Recreation/Northfield-Brook-Lake/

Located: 1550 Northfield Road, RT. 254 Thomaston, CT.

The Plymouth Reservoir

PLYMOUTH RESERVOIR

Just over the line between Thomaston and Plymouth rests the beautiful Plymouth Reservoir. When you pull into the small parking area, you'll immediately notice the vast views and woodsy surroundings. From there, you can step right out onto the dock and feel as though you're on a ship, floating on the water. Fish are easily spied from the dock, and you can also launch your kayak here to further explore the water and woods. Hiking trails surround the lake and extend out, and it's even rumored that the famous Leatherman had a cave in these woods, which you can visit by taking a specific trail.

Because the reservoir is not a state park, it is open year-round, although there are signs to keep out during the winter months when the water freezes.

Website:

https://plymouthct.myrec.com/info/facilities/details.aspx?FacilityID=11629

Located: Route 8 Thomaston, to Route 6, to North Street, Plymouth, CT.

Thomaston Restaurants and Food

Cutie Pies (cupcakes, cakes, baked goods)

131 Main Street #105a

Cutiepiesct.com

Senor Pancho's (Mexican food, sit-down dining)

360 Watertown Rd

Senorpanchosthomaston.com

Crabby Al's (sit-down dining, seafood, water views)

157 East Main Street

Crabbyals.com

Chubba's (breakfast, salads, sandwiches)

76 Watertown Rd.

Scoop it Up (ice cream)

102 East Main Street

Rozzi's Restaurant (homestyle, burgers, breakfast)

265 Watertown Road

Rozzisrestaurant.com/

Clocktown Brewing Company (pizza, burgers, salads)

Inside the Historic Seth Thomas Clock Factory

135 South Main Street

clocktownbrewingco.com

Thomaston Family Diner (daily specials, sandwiches, soups)

381 S Main Street

Patti's Place (Diner food, daily specials, a town favorite!)

4 Park Street

Facebook: Patti's Place of Thomaston

Black Rock Tavern (Burgers, Sandwiches, Salads)

78 Main Street

Blackrocktavern.com

Mona Lisa Ristorante (pizza, grinders, pasta)

66 Main Street

Monalisaristorante.net

Hometown Pizza (pizza, Italian)

299 South Main Street

Facebook: Hometown Thomaston

Milestone Wood Fired Pizza (New Haven style pizza)

68 East Main Street

Milestonepizzatruck.com

Thomaston Shopping

Adams Grocery Store
92 Main Street

Thomaston Feed (pet supplies)
141 Watertown Rd.
Thomastonfeed.com

Red's Hardware
32 Main Street
Facebook: Red's Hardware

Buell's Florist
81 E Main Street
Abuellsthomastonflorist.com

Antiques at the Green (just over the line Thomaston/Plymouth)
Crafts, unique gifts, and antiques
703 Main Street, Plymouth, CT

Clevelands' Country Store (Plymouth)
food, ice cream, deli, and specialty items
655 Main Street Plymouth, CT
Clevelandscountrystore.com

Foster's Farm Market (produce, flowers, seasonal items)
11 Waterbury Road

Roma Florist and Greenhouses (flowers for all occasions)
26 Center Street
romafloristandgreenhouses.com

Litchfield Center Stores (10-minute drive)
toys, art and antiques, home decor, food/restaurants
Located along the historic Litchfield Green
West Street, Litchfield CT.

The Dutch Epicure Shop, LLC (Litchfield)
gourmet food from Holland (Hagel, specialty cheeses, candy, and more)
491 Bantam Rd. Litchfield, CT.
dutchepicure.com

The Litchfield Candy Company (Litchfield)
Assorted chocolate and candy: gourmet, seasonal, and nostalgic
245 West Street Litchfield, CT

Thomaston Events

Light up Thomaston

Main Street, Thomaston

November (takes place the Saturday after Thanksgiving, typically 6pm)

Santa Claus

Holiday Parade

Christmas Tree Raffle

Live Music

Horse and Carriage Rides

Carnival Rides

Food and Drink

Thomaston Fireman's Carnival and Fireworks Show

Late July or Early August

Carnival Rides

Fireworks

Parade

More Listings on Facebook: Thomaston CT Happenings

Surrounding Areas

The Carousel Museum (museum, Bristol, CT)
95 Riverside Ave Bristol, CT.
Thecarouselmuseum.org

American Clock and Watch Museum (museum, Bristol, CT)
100 Maple Street Bristol, CT
Clockandwatchmuseum.org

Lake Compounce (amusement park, Bristol, CT)
185 Enterprise Drive Bristol, CT
Lakecompounce.com

Antiques on the Farmington (antiques, Collinsville, CT)
10 Depot Street Collinsville (Canton), CT
Antiquesonthefarmington.com

Bristol Street Press

Bristolstreetpress.com

inquiries@bristolstreetpress.com

Made in the USA
Middletown, DE
08 September 2021